The Kehoe Lecture in Irish History 2018

Suffrage and citizenship in Ireland, 1912–18

Senia Pašeta

LONDON
INSTITUTE OF HISTORICAL RESEARCH

Published by

UNIVERSITY OF LONDON
SCHOOL OF ADVANCED STUDY
INSTITUTE OF HISTORICAL RESEARCH
Senate House, Malet Street, London WC1E 7HU

2019

ISBN 978-1-912702-18-3 (PDF edition)
ISBN 978-1-912702-31-2 (paperback edition)

DOI
10.14296/119.9781912702183

Senia Pašeta is professor of modern history at the University of Oxford and a fellow of St Hugh's College, Oxford. A specialist in the history of late nineteenth- and early twentieth-century Ireland, Senia's current research focuses on women's political activism and on connections between Irish and British radical politics. Her publications include *Irish Nationalist Women, 1900–1918* (Cambridge, 2013) and *Uncertain Futures: Essays about the Irish Past* (Oxford, 2016).

The Kehoe Lecture in Irish History is one of the principal named lectures hosted each year by the Institute of Historical Research, University of London. Inaugurated in 2016, the Kehoe Lecture promotes new research undertaken by leading scholars of Irish history and culture.

Suffrage and citizenship in Ireland, 1912–18

Senia Pašeta

**Presented on 15 November 2018 at the
Institute of Historical Research, University of London**

All Irish historians and anyone interested in Irish history will know that we have for some time been in the middle of a decade of centenaries. Beginning in around 2012 to coincide with the centenary of the introduction to the third Home Rule Bill, we saw a peak of activity in 2016. There is a lot more to come, especially as we head towards the centenary of partition and the creation of the Irish Free State and Northern Ireland. And there will be many interesting pit stops along the way: quite how the beginning of the War of Independence will be marked in the context of Brexit, for example, is anyone's guess.

This specifically Irish commemorating has intersected in some ways with the centenary of the First World War, which has particular intellectual and political resonances for early twentieth-century Ireland and its historians, and for the ongoing peace process. In 2018 we've also been celebrating or at least marking the centenary of women's suffrage whose commemoration has similarly lent itself to contemporary political concerns and campaigns including #metoo and timesup. In my own way I've been involved in all three of these commemorations in the UK and in Ireland, in a number of academic and non-academic contexts. I have found these instructive and fascinating, not least because of the ways in which women as historical actors and subjects (not to mention scholars) have been integrated – or otherwise – in them.

I've also been struck by the degree to which these three circles of commemoration – war, revolution and suffrage – have been thematically integrated. My own research intersects with all three. How could it not as I argue that the impact on Irish politics of feminism in the early twentieth century was profound. Feminist ideas shaped some aspects of Irish nationalism itself in the period in such obvious and important ways that it seems incredible to me that this has not been more widely recognized, let alone accepted. Feminism as a movement in early twentieth-century Ireland was diverse, but its most public and recognizable articulations were firmly embedded in the suffrage demand and this will be the focus of this lecture.

1

I

The impact of the First World War on suffrage has long been established as an idea which has attained real currency. The idea that women were 'given' the vote because of their war service seems to have been widely accepted. It is interesting that the main way in which women's suffrage has attained a place in the story of 1914–18 is through this idea of women's 'service' being 'rewarded' by a grateful nation (the nation presumably being male). This is less the case in Ireland, partly because the notion that service in the First World War should be rewarded is controversial to say the least, but also because of the ongoing reluctance to integrate women's political activism into the revolutionary story, except in quite formulaic ways. Additionally, the Irish suffrage movement is especially challenging. Although its supporters ranged across the political spectrum, so too did its critics. Constitutional nationalists and unionists criticized suffragists for prioritizing sex over nation, particularly at points of constitutional crisis; advanced nationalists including Sinn Feiners accused suffragists of prostrating themselves before a foreign parliament and therefore of recognizing its legitimacy, while some trade unionists remained suspicious of the campaign's middle-class nature. As in Britain, accusations of hysteria and ineptitude were not restricted to any one political view.

A further complicating factor was that the Irish suffrage movement in its broadest sense was genuinely unlike any other political movement in the country. Although individual suffragists had their own views on the national question, a real attempt to remain non-party political meant that they could and did co-operate primarily as feminists rather than as unionists or nationalists. Early twentieth-century suffragists knew that this position was neither easy nor popular, but they did nonetheless – at times – manage to create a movement for democratic change which consisted of nationalists and unionists, Protestants and Catholics, women from all the provinces and from across the UK. For this they were vilified as they knew they would be; but, in this, they were also unrivalled.

I want to discuss here this corralling of women's suffrage – as a movement and a research subject in its own right – in both Irish and British historiography. And I want to argue that our understanding of modern Irish and British politics would be enormously enriched if we recognized two things: that the Irish and British suffrage movements were deeply connected; and that the women's suffrage movement across the UK was shaped in fundamental ways by the Irish Question from the late nineteenth century and into the twentieth. In other words, the women's suffrage movement did not exist in a political vacuum. It interacted with, influenced and was influenced by the other main political questions of the day, and with *the* main political question of the day – Ireland.

The women's suffrage and Irish questions had much in common. Not only did they reach their political zeniths at around the same time, they both aimed to challenge the British constitution in radical ways and to expand the categories of political citizenship. In their focus on constitutional change, they operated within a longer political tradition which included Catholic emancipation, Chartism and the Labour Party, all of which similarly sought radical change through parliamentary means. Irish nationalists since Daniel O'Connell had mastered the art of pursuing constitutional change alongside an implicit threat of violence. At times this implicit violence would become explicit such as during the Land War of the 1870s and 1880s, but constitutional change remained its primary focus. British suffragettes would adopt this very strategy and make it their own.

There are a number of ways in which one could explore the many connections between the British suffrage movement and Ireland or more specifically the Irish Question in this period. We could, for example, undertake a biographical study of the many Irish women who were active in the British suffrage movement. Women including Helen Blackburn, author, activist and joint editor of the *Englishwomen's Review*; Frances Power Cobb, writer and one of the best known suffragists of her day; Laura Geraldine Lennox, a Cork native, Women's Social and Political Union (WSPU) activist, editor, suffrage prisoner and hunger striker; or even Eva Gore Booth, socialist and suffragist, and sister of Constance Markievicz. There are many, many more. The influence of Irish women on the British suffrage movement is a story waiting to be told and it's a story about the broader movement of politically liberal and often educated Irish women to Britain in this period.

One could also look at the formal links between the Irish and British suffrage movements, beginning in the mid nineteenth century and enduring into the twentieth, and how those cross-British Isles and UK collaborations shaped the suffrage movements on both sides of the Irish Sea. Though fraught at times, they were important especially in the early days when the Irish movement was small and found strategic and political strength through its alliances with British organizations. During these formative years, the vast majority of Irish suffragists were Protestants, of whom many were Quakers. This shared Protestantism helped to bind English and Irish campaigners whose common faith often also informed their philanthropic and reformist activities. Given that most of the prominent early Irish suffragists – like Isabella Tod in Belfast and Anna Haslam in Dublin – were also unionists, their views about social and political reform were articulated

Figure 1. Poster and admission ticket for Christabel Pankhurst's lecture at the Rotunda, Dublin, 11 March 1910 © National Library of Ireland.

in both Irish and more broadly liberal British terms.

We could also fruitfully explore the longer history of tension between the British and Irish women's movements which was evident in different ways from the late nineteenth century. Some historians have in fact studied this, albeit usually from the perspective of the damage caused by the English suffragettes who interfered in Ireland for their own misguided reasons and with little sense of the particular dynamics of the Irish suffrage movement. And they have a point. However, co-operation across the British Isles was evident too and, once again, contingent on wider political developments. Focusing too closely on disagreements between the Irish and British suffrage movements runs the risk of over simplifying a complex dynamic on a number of levels.

I am now going to look at how the suffrage and Irish questions interacted in important ways, and what studying these can tell us about both, as well as about the broader political context of the period. And I'll be concentrating especially on the years 1910 to 1914, when the Irish and suffrage questions intersected like never before as feminist and nationalist demands competed most obviously and damagingly for parliamentary time and attention. The purpose of this is not merely to highlight some under-researched aspects of women's history in Britain and Ireland, though that is important, but also to situate both campaigns in their wider political contexts and to try to expand our understanding of the interconnectedness of these reform movements.

II

As I have already suggested, British suffrage and feminist interest in Irish affairs had a long pedigree. This was partly driven by a sense that the parallels between the Irish Question and women's suffrage were evident, but it was also due to the more basic fact that suffragists were frequently deeply interested in political questions beyond suffrage. Given that British feminists were fundamentally driven by political aims and that many were involved in a multitude of campaigning organizations, it is not surprising that a number of them also became involved in the Home Rule debate from the 1880s. As the Irish Question and women's suffrage came to pose the two most significant challenges to the British constitution over the next thirty years, their connection became if not inevitable, then at least unsurprising. Gladstonian Home Rule cut across the women's movement in the UK just as it did the Liberal Party to which so many suffragists were aligned, sending some of them into the Unionist fold.

When the Liberal Party split over Home Rule, most pro-suffrage radicals remained loyal to Gladstone, despite his own opposition to women's suffrage. These included Ursula and Jacob Bright and Richard and Emmeline Pankhurst. Other suffragists who adopted the Gladstonian line came to think about the women's suffrage demand in a different, more complex constitutional context as a by-product. The best known of these was Josephine Butler who argued in sometimes strikingly Gladstonian language that the Irish Question tested the Christian faith of the British people.[1] Butler's advocacy of Irish devolution was based on a combination of her reading of Irish history, the democratic will as expressed by the Irish people and, most interestingly, on a broader theory of political justice in which Irish Catholics and women featured. Other well-known liberal women also took up the cause, arguing the nationalist case in committees, in drawing rooms and at public meetings. This is an aspect of liberal culture in Britain and Ireland we know very little about, but it was a thriving and important one.

As both the suffrage and the Irish Home Rule campaigns developed into the twentieth century, the connections drawn between them became more explicit and more powerful. As one campaigner argued, 'two analogous movements [suffrage and Irish nationalism] like all those making for human freedom, ought, of course, to advance together'.[2] Not all suffragists agreed, but relationships between British and Irish suffragists and suffragettes

---

[1] J. Butler, *Our Christianity Tested by the Irish Question* (London, 1887).
[2] *Freeman's Journal*, 10 Apr. 1912, p. 9.

Figure 2. Members of the Irish Women's Franchise League, Hyde Park, London, 21 June 1908; centre (in white with sash) Laura Geraldine Lennox, with Hanna Sheehy Skeffington to her left. Courtesy of Dublin City Library & Archive.

remained very productive. Irish women, for example, often joined the great suffrage marches in London.

The Irish contingents consisted of mixed groups of women including prominent unionists, most notably Dr Elizabeth Bell, a unionist member of the Belfast Irish Women's Suffrage Society. Other participants had excellent nationalist pedigrees; these included Louise Gavan Duffy, Miss O'Connell and Miss O'Connell Hayes – 'granddaughters of the Liberator' – wives and daughters of nationalist MPs including Mrs Hugh Law, and Mary, Kathleen and Hannah Sheehy, daughters of David Sheehy MP who had himself been imprisoned during the Land War.[3]

Irish women joined London protests for the obvious reason that Westminster alone had the power to grant them the vote, and they also joined for reasons of solidarity. But some also travelled in order to participate in militancy before it had begun in Ireland. Thirteen members of the Irish Women's Franchise League (IWFL) were imprisoned for their involvement in WSPU-organized marches and associated disturbances between 1910 and May 1912, while several other Irish women who were resident in Britain or not members of the IWFL were similarly active.[4]

---

[3] *Votes for Women*, 24 June 1910, p. 18.
[4] *Irish Citizen*, 25 May 1912, p. 8.

Figure 3. Members of the Irish contingent of the Women's
Coronation Procession, London, June 1911; Laura Geraldine Lennox
stands on the right (with sash). © Museum of London.

Close co-operation was possible because of the connections between the Irish and British movement, often facilitated by women like Laura Geraldine Lennox who served as an intermediary between the WSPU and the Irish Women's Franchise League.[5] Co-operation went the other way too. English suffragists including the Pankhursts and Millicent Fawcett were also frequent visitors to Ireland while Irish suffragists were avid readers of the British suffrage press, especially before the foundation of their own suffrage newspaper, the *Irish Citizen* in 1912.

Nonetheless, with very few exceptions, Irish feminists of all political persuasions maintained that they should be left to run their own affairs. Consequently the direct involvement of English organizations was frowned upon. This helps to explain why so few British societies established active Irish branches. There were exceptions but they were thin on the ground and Ireland hosted a large range of suffrage groups, some of which were quite small and stand-alone societies, many of them spearheaded by very

[5] I am very grateful to Karen Fitzgerald for the information about Laura Geraldine Lennox which she generously shared with me for this lecture.

7

energetic organizers in towns and cities including Waterford, Cork, Newry and Lisburn.[6]

An *Irish Citizen* editorial argued in 1912 that 'we believe that the rousing of the Irish people had best be left to Irish women, who understand the psychology of their countrymen as the ablest English advocate never can'.[7] This view seemed to have been accepted by all British suffrage societies before 1912, which had maintained good relationships with the Irish suffrage groups but did not interfere directly in Irish affairs. The *Citizen* had produced this editorial in response to the direct involvement of English members of the WSPU in Irish politics on Irish soil in July 1912. In Dublin on that occasion, one WSPU member had thrown a hatchet into a carriage transporting the British prime minister, Herbert Asquith, and John Redmond, Parnellite leader of the Irish Parliamentary Party (IPP), while another had tried to set fire to the theatre in which they were due to appear. This was a new and alarming development which tested the limits of co-operation between Irish and British suffragists. Sylvia Pankhurst, subsequently a critic of the WSPU's Irish strategy, later conceded that although Irish women were 'active and vigilant', 'the WSPU would not leave the Irish Question to them'. When a Conciliation Bill was defeated in 1912, Christabel Pankhurst sent a poster parade to parliament, bearing the message: 'NO VOTES FOR WOMEN: NO HOME RULE'.[8]

How had it come to this? Why were English suffragettes targeting MPs in Ireland by 1912 when they had not previously done so? This change in tactics was mainly a response to a series of parliamentary defeats for women's suffrage for which Irish nationalist MPs were held accountable. Many British campaigners came to believe, as Christabel Pankhurst would argue, that 'Mr Redmond and the Nationalist Members are to a large extent the arbiters of the political fate of English women',[9] and their direct involvement in Irish political life deepened as a result.

This had become evident from 1910 when Irish nationalist MPs effectively held the balance of power at Westminster. After winning the 1906 election in a landslide, the Liberal Party's majority was so reduced over two elections in 1910 that it became dependent on its Irish and Labour allies to get through its ambitious legislative programme. In practical terms this meant that the IPP had real leverage and could make demands in return for its support. The IPP's main demand was of course a parliamentary Home Rule Bill. At

---

[6] E. Crawford, *The Women's Suffrage Movement in Britain and Ireland: a Regional Study* (London, 2006), pp. 262–3.

[7] *Irish Citizen*, 14 Sept. 1912, p. 130.

[8] S. Pankhurst, *The Suffragette Movement* (London, 1931, reprinted 1988), p. 403.

[9] *The Suffragette*, 3 Oct. 1913, p. 880.

the same time, the women's suffrage campaign had reached a new stage in 1910 as MPs from all the parties, including several from the IPP, organized collectively in a Conciliation Committee with the aim of getting through a cross-party suffrage bill. The suffrage question was not a party one in so far as no party supported it as policy. The exception was the Labour Party, but its first loyalty was to manhood suffrage and it supported votes for women as part of a broader electoral reform package. Each party, including the IPP, was divided on the question so lobbying took place across the political spectrum.

Calculating precisely how many MPs within each party were pro-suffrage is difficult, but the IPP had a good record on suffrage in the Commons and was seen as friendly by many suffragists. In 1912 the Labour politician Philip Snowden claimed that the IPP had 'contributed a larger share of votes in favour of woman suffrage than any other party except the Labour Party' and my own calculations bear out his analysis.[10] Suffragists close to the IPP argued that at least three quarters of members were sympathetic to the cause and that there was 'no substantial opposition' in the IPP to women's suffrage.[11] A majority of nationalist MPs voted for Conciliation Bills in both 1910 and 1911. The 1911 vote was emphatic as it was won by the huge margin of 255 to eighty-eight, not least because of the support of a clear majority of nationalist MPs.[12]

But the most urgent test would come in 1912 when the next reading of the Conciliation Bill, widely expected to pass, was debated and very narrowly defeated by only fourteen votes in March 1912. The nationalist vote was decisive as none voted for it, thirty-five voted against and forty abstained.[13] Suffragists widely believed that 'had the nationalists been true to their principles instead of sacrificing them to political expediency the bill would have been carried'.[14] There were in fact a number of reasons for its defeat, but suffragists generally agreed that 'the Irish Party killed the Conciliation Bill'.[15]

Irish MPs voted in this way in order to free up parliamentary time which they believed could be better used on passing the third Home Rule Bill. It was also believed that no risk should be taken to split the Liberal Party or worse, the cabinet, on the eve of the parliamentary Home Rule debate. This may have been true but it offered little solace to suffragists and the fact

---

[10] C. Rover, *Women's Suffrage and Party Politics in Britain, 1866–1914* (London, 1967), p. 155.
[11] *Irish Times*, 18 Oct. 1911, p. 5.
[12] *Common Cause*, 11 May 1911, p. 80.
[13] *Common Cause*, 4 Apr. 1912, p. 884.
[14] *Common Cause*, 4 Apr. 1912, p. 879.
[15] *Irish Citizen*, 25 May 1912, p. 1.

Figure 4. John Redmond, 'the New Liberator', denies the rights of women, *The Irish Citizen*, 15 March 1913. Courtesy of Dublin City Public Library and Archive.

that the IPP's leader John Redmond was a known anti-suffragist did not help. Irish suffragists in particular held him personally responsible for the nationalist vote.

Irish suffragettes increasingly took direct action by attempting to attend nationalist events at which they were unwelcome throughout 1912. There were of course a great many such public meetings held to discuss the Home Rule Bill and feelings often ran very high at such gatherings. Feminists, even known nationalists, found that they were often refused entrance or worse, forcefully evicted and brutally treated for what were perceived to be their attempts to 'kill Home Rule'. Worse was to come when the IPP held its annual convention in April 1912. About seventy women marched to the convention and almost all of them, even those like Patricia Hoey who were connected officially with the United Irish League, were prevented from entering the Mansion House.[16] A final attempt to sway the IPP was made at a mass suffrage meeting held in Dublin in June 1912, this time to urge the inclusion of women's suffrage in the Home Rule Bill then under discussion. Hanna Sheehy Skeffington claimed that the exclusion of women from the Home Rule Bill had drawn together militant and constitutionalist, and nationalist and unionist, and that the party allegiances 'so dear to our loyal women' were 'for once subordinated to sex principle'.[17] This meeting represented a remarkable show of unity in the context of an ever-widening chasm between North and South, unionist and nationalist, militant and constitutionalist, and this did not come easily to some women.[18] When cabinet ministers and Irish MPs failed to reply to a resolution which called on the government to amend the Home Rule Bill to enfranchise women on the basis of the local government register, the IWFL took up militancy for the first time in Ireland. On 13 June eight members were arrested for breaking windows in government buildings in Dublin. All the women went to gaol having refused to pay a fine.[19]

The final 1912 showdown came when Philip Snowden introduced an amendment to the Home Rule Bill which would enfranchise women on the local government register. The Irish MPs maintained that they had an absolutely free vote on Snowden's amendment, as they had always enjoyed on women's suffrage bills. However, this was difficult to square with the fact that when the vote was finally taken 'the division was not on party lines except so far as the Irish Nationalists were concerned'.[20]

The women's suffrage issue placed nationalist suffragist MPs in a very awkward situation, not least because they were forced to deny what was for many of them a very strongly held principle. Nonetheless, Home Rule was their priority. As Hugh Law, a committed supporter and member of the Conciliation Committee, told the House: 'at the present moment I am convinced that among Irish women themselves there is no such demand as should justify us in imperilling Home Rule even in the very slightest degree in order to extend the franchise to them'.[21] The Labour leader Ramsay MacDonald understood this, expressing sympathy for Law who, he claimed, was 'in an extremely difficult position. He would like to vote one way and he cannot. He is going to vote the other way and he wants an excuse for it'.[22]

[16] *Irish Citizen*, 1 June 1912, p. 9.
[17] *Irish Citizen*, 1 June 1912, p. 9.
[18] *Irish Citizen*, 15 June 1912, p. 29.
[19] *Irish Citizen*, 4 January 1913, p. 261.
[20] *Irish Independent*, 6 Nov. 1912, p. 7.
[21] Hansard, *Parliamentary Debates*, 5th ser., xliii (5 Nov. 1912), col. 1115.
[22] Hansard, *Parliamentary Debates*, 5th ser., xliii (5 Nov. 1912), col. 1117.

This infuriated Irish feminists and was seen as a serious betrayal by British women who believed that the franchise arrangements enshrined in the 1912 Home Rule Bill would be nothing less than a precedent for the rest of the UK. This really mattered, especially as many thought that Irish Home Rule constituted little more than an expanded form of local government. As women across the UK had been enfranchised for local elections since the late nineteenth century, they therefore believed themselves entitled to a vote in any new form of local government, no matter how advanced or evolved. But conceding this interpretation of the Home Rule Bill was anathema to Irish nationalist MPs who could hardly agree that decades of hard campaigning had resulted merely in an elaborate form of local government.

At the same time, nationalist MPs remained reluctant to spell out precisely what kind of political autonomy Home Rule had delivered after many years of struggle. Irish parliamentary nationalism had long been characterized by calculated ambiguity on the question of what settlement it was prepared to accept from any British government. The importance to the suffrage argument of the distinction between domestic and imperial parliaments has been curiously under-explored by historians, though to contemporaries on all sides of the argument it was crucial, just as it was to suffrage campaigners.[23]

Suffrage campaigners played upon this uncertainty. One of the most interesting files I have come across in my research is in the National Union of Women's Suffrage Societies archive held in the Women's Library. In the run up to the vote on Philip Snowden's amendment, the National Union produced several versions of a letter asking MPs to vote for it. They tailored their letters to the individual views of each MP on suffrage and played on various of their prejudices. They even tried to convince anti-suffrage and anti-Home Rule MPs to vote for the amendment because it suggested that the new Irish parliament would be nothing more than a local government body and this would be a seen as an insult to the Irish Nationalist Party.[24]

The Snowden amendment was blocked by the same forces that had defeated the Conciliation Bill in March. Plans to amend the government's Manhood Suffrage Bill to include women were scuppered in early 1913, and campaigners were forced to resign themselves to the fact that there was no real chance of a women's suffrage bill passing before the next general election which had to take place no later than December 1915.

[23] S. Pašeta, *Irish Nationalist Women, 1900–1918* (Cambridge, 2013), pp. 86–8.
[24] The Women's Library, London School of Economics, 2LSW/C/5/3, Conciliation Bill and Philip Snowden's amendment to Home Rule Bill, 1912.

III

This was very bad news for suffragists and suffragettes, but Ireland once again provided new opportunities to push forward, this time courtesy of unionists who gave feminists a model of political organization, and more importantly, powerful evidence of political double standards and of the effectiveness of militancy. Suffragists asked frequently why it was that the rights of unionists and Protestants within a future Home Rule Ireland were being protected and catered for, while women's rights were dismissed.[25] More pointedly, Emmeline Pankhurst asked:

> We heard prominent members of Parliament openly declaring that if the Home Rule bill was passed, Ulster would fight and Ulster would be right. None of these men were arrested. Instead they were applauded ... What does this all mean? Why is it that men's blood-shedding militancy is applauded and women's symbolic militancy punished with a prison cell and the forcible feeding horror ... If it is right for men to fight for their freedom, and God knows what the human race would be like to-day if men had not, since time began, fought for their freedom, then it is right for women to fight for their freedom and the freedom of the children they bear. On this declaration of faith the militant women of England rest their case.[26]

They seemed to have a point: the parallels here between Ulster unionism and militant suffrage were evident. The unionist response to impending Home Rule had been swift and resolute. Its governing body, the Ulster Unionist Council was well organized and pledged at once to resist Home Rule. Militancy formed a crucial part of this agenda and was evident from about 1910, confirmed by the formation of the Ulster Volunteer Force (UVF) in 1913, a paramilitary organization established to resist Home Rule by violent means if necessary. It attracted around 90,000 members and engaged in successful gun running and military training for its unionist militia. Women too were heavily involved, forming the Ulster Women's Unionist Council in 1911 and mobilizing in large numbers. The Women's Unionist Council had an estimated membership of 115,000 to 200,000 making it easily the largest women's group in Ireland, if not the entire UK.[27]

The UVF's success and seeming immunity from official censure inspired a nationalist imitator in the Irish Volunteers, established in 1913, to protect the Home Rule Bill. But it also inspired suffragettes and suffragists who

---

[25] *The Suffragette*, 23 May 1913, p. 526; 27 June 1913, p. 612; *Votes for Women*, 3 Nov. 1911, p. 68; 12 Apr. 1912, p. 438.

[26] E. Pankhurst, *My Own Story* (London, 1914), pp. 267–9.

[27] D. Urquhart, *Women in Ulster Politics, 1890–1940* (Dublin, 2000), p. 61.

The Suffragette, September 19, 1913.

The Suffragette

Edited by Christabel Pankhurst

The Official Organ of the Women's Social and Political Union.

Registered at the G.P.O. as a Newspaper.

No. 49—Vol. I.   FRIDAY, SEPTEMBER 19, 1913.   Price 1d. Weekly (Post Free)

VOTES FOR ULSTER WOMEN.

IT is announced that women are to vote for the Ulster Parliament to be created by Sir Edward Carson and his colleagues.

This announcement is a proof recently of the great advance in power and influence that women have made of late, and especially during the past few months of militancy.

The decision on the part of the Ulster men to share their political rights with women is also an illustration of the fact that the Government, and the Liberal-Labour-Nationalist Coalition which supports them, are far less Liberal in thought and in deed than are their political opponents of the Anti-Home Rule party.

When the Ulster men talk of freedom for Ulster, they mean freedom for women as well as for men. When the Government and their supporters talk of freedom for Ireland and Home Rule, they mean freedom for men only and Home Rule for men only.

It is for women now to hold fast to the victory they have achieved in Ulster.

There is talk of possible compromise between Home Rulers and the opponents of Home Rule. If such a compromise should come, the Women's Social and Political Union will fight with all its strength to ensure that in the compromise women's right to vote shall not be sacrificed.

There must be no compromise nor any other settlement of the Irish question, except upon the basis of Votes for Women.

Figure 5. *The Suffragette,* 13 September 1913.

looked on in dismay to question why suffragettes were 'arrested, imprisoned and tortured while the militant men of Ulster go free'?[28]

The stakes were raised still higher when the Unionist leader, Edward Carson, announced the foundation of a provisional government for Ulster in September 1913. The Ulster Women's Unionist Council was informed that the draft articles of the provisional government would in fact enfranchise women on the basis of the local government register, and that women would be invited to sit on various committees established under the aegis of the provisional government.[29]

The WSPU launched an 'Ulster campaign' and quickly moved to take the credit for the Unionist Party's 'conversion'. The foundations for this shift had been laid before the English organization had intervened, and a number

[28] *The Suffragette,* 23 May 1913, p. 526.
[29] *Belfast Newsletter,* 12 Sept. 1913, p. 7.

of Irish activists similarly claimed credit for the announcement. Whoever was responsible, the fact remained that as far as feminists were concerned, women's suffrage had at last been conceded within the UK.[30] The WSPU quickly declared war on the Liberal government and the Irish Nationalist Party, announcing that its policy would henceforth be 'to do everything possible to prevent the voting rights which Ulster men are conceding to women being taken away from them by the Liberal government'.[31] This in effect meant opposing Home Rule on Irish soil and upping its militant campaign in Ireland.

The WSPU established a Belfast branch and Dublin and Cork branches soon followed. The majority of Irish suffrage organizations opposed the involvement of the WSPU in Irish matters, some because they were anti-militant, and others because they believed that Irish suffragists should be left 'to work out their own salvation'.[32] The IWFL objected because the WSPU was 'not Irish',[33] while the Northern Committee of the Irishwomen's Suffrage Federation put 'on record' its 'disapproval of the policy of the Women's Social and Political Union in Ulster', explaining that the WSPU was 'an English association, and ha[d] no connection with any Irish suffrage organisation'.[34] Suffrage societies around the country agreed with their analysis, especially after the WSPU began to engage in a programme of systematic militancy in Ireland. Leading members of the Munster Women's Franchise League raged at the 'sheer madness' of the WSPU's strategy of 'anti-Home Rule cum militancy', especially when it threatened to send an organizer to Cork. Susan Day of the Munster Women's Franchise League explained to fellow member, Edith Somerville that:

> If the WSPU persist, the Irish societies will only have the very unpleasant task of repudiating them as thoroughly as possible. I have a great deal of sympathy with the English militants, but our first consideration is for our own country and it is infuriating to think of the crass English ignorance of the Irish affairs that is inflating the WSPU, provoking them in this imbecile campaign, which will do us infinite harm just at the moment when we are beginning to pull ourselves together.[35]

---

[30] *The Suffragette*, 20 Sept. 1913, p. 843.
[31] *The Suffragette*, 20 Sept. 1913, p. 843.
[32] *Irish Citizen*, 20 Sept. 1913, p. 145.
[33] *Irish Citizen*, 20 Sept. 1913, p. 141.
[34] *Northern Whig*, 14 Apr. 1914.
[35] University College Dublin Archives, P48a/8(4), Mary MacSwiney Papers, Edith Somerville to Susan Day (6 Oct. 1913) and Susan Day to Edith Somerville (no date).

But the WSPU had other ideas, insisting that as far as it was concerned, 'there ought not to be a distinction between the English Movement and the Irish Movement any more than there is a distinction between the English Movement and the Scottish Movement'.[36]

The arrival of the WSPU added further complexity to the already complex dynamics of the Irish suffrage movement. Notwithstanding Emmeline Pankhurst's simplistic analysis of the Scottish comparison, the context in which Irish women campaigned for citizenship rights *was* different from the British environment. Not only were Irish women obliged to deal with their own MPs who were allied with the major British parties but followed their own agendas, they also operated in a more unstable political environment which was characterized by deep national and religious fissures as well as division on the women's suffrage question itself. The WSPU's largely unwelcome involvement further complicated matters and increased tensions within the Irish movement.

The optimism engendered by the Unionist Council's declaration soon faded as it failed to elaborate on its original promise. Suffragists became increasingly anxious about the pledge whose fulfilment looked ever more unlikely as the weeks passed. By March 1914 the WSPU announced the end of its support for Edward Carson, declaring war on his party unless it honoured the pledge.[37] It didn't. A new period of militancy followed, with an intensive arson campaign alienating the Ulster public and seeing thirteen women arrested for suffrage activities in a six-month period from March 1914.[38]

The outbreak of the First World War, as we know, changed everything. It probably averted civil war in Ireland and it threw suffrage societies into a period of deliberation about their own response to the European hostilities. Historians have continued to be intrigued by the response of the WSPU to the war and to ask how and why its militant, sometimes violent and illegal political activism and anti-government lobbying and agitation became patriotic, law abiding and pacific. Such an about turn is often seen as unprecedented and quite bizarre. But of course it was no such thing for the Ulster Unionists, male and female, had – not for the first time – behaved in exactly the same way on the announcement of war. Once again, the men and women who most vigorously tested the British constitution across the UK demonstrated that loyalty and citizenship rights were both complex and conditional.

---

[36] Sheehy Skeffington Papers, National Library of Ireland, MS 22,664, Emmeline Pankhurst to Hanna Sheehy Skeffington (26 Sept. 1913).

[37] D. Urquhart, '"An articulate and definite cry for political freedom": the Ulster suffrage movement', *Women's History Review*, xi (2002), pp. 283–4.

[38] Urquhart, *Women in Ulster Politics*, p. 36.

I have only begun to scratch the surface of the story of these complex relationships between Irish and British suffrage movements and ideas, not to mention the intriguing parallels between the suffrage and Irish questions. The longer term impact of these connections was profound, especially in Ireland where the IPP's implosion at the 1918 general election – in which Irish women voted and an Irish suffragist and republican became the first woman elected as an MP – owed much to its utter failure to support women's suffrage and to cultivate a serious women's association, just as every other major political party had by this time. While unionist and Sinn Fein women mobilized, canvassed and organized on behalf of their candidates, the IPP had no such support network to fall back on. Instead, its candidates faced an open campaign of feminist opposition from women who persisted in reminding it that 'women were more than lunatics and imbeciles; they were citizens of Ireland, and they had tenacious memories'.[39]

Karen Offen has argued that 'Feminist claims are primarily political claims, not philosophical claims. They never arise in – or respond to – a sociological vacuum. They are put forward in concrete settings and they pose explicit political demands for change'.[40] This is especially pertinent to this period of Irish and British history. The history of feminism in Ireland and Britain must be understood in the context of Ireland's broader history of political change, and a study of political change in Ireland in this period should take feminist political activism firmly into account. Neither was unaffected by the other and both had a profound impact on the history of political activism and change in nineteenth- and twentieth-century Britain and Ireland.

---

[39] *Irish Independent*, 10 Dec. 1918, p. 4.
[40] K. Offen, *European Feminisms: a Political History* (Stanford, Calif., 2000), p. xv.

INSTITUTE OF | SCHOOL OF
HISTORICAL | ADVANCED STUDY
RESEARCH | UNIVERSITY
OF LONDON

The Institute of Historical Research (IHR) is the UK's national centre for history. Founded in 1921, the Institute facilitates and promotes innovative research via its primary collections library, and its programme of training, publishing, conferences, seminars and fellowships. The IHR is one of the nine humanities research institutes of the School of Advanced Study at the University of London.

'IHR Shorts' is a new Open Access publishing series from the Institute of Historical Research at the University of London. Insightful and concise, IHR Shorts offer incisive commentaries on contemporary historical debates. Titles typically range from 15,000 to 50,000 words with a focus on interdisciplinary approaches to the past.

1. Dethroning historical reputations: universities, museums and the commemoration of benefactors
   edited by Jill Pellew and Lawrence Goldman (2018)

2. Magna Carta: history, context and influence
   edited by Lawrence Goldman (2018)

3. Suffrage and citizenship in Ireland, 1912–18 (The Kehoe Lecture in Irish History 2018)
   Senia Pašeta (2019)

Lightning Source UK Ltd.
Milton Keynes UK
UKHW020400290921
391325UK00003B/11